Honor in Teaching: Reflections

Honor in Teaching: Reflections

Marcella L. Kysilka, Editor

Kappa Delta Pi Publications
West Lafayette, Indiana
1990

Library of Congress Cataloging-in-Publication Data

Honor in teaching.

    Includes bibliographical references.

    1. Teaching--Vocational guidance--United States. 2.
Teachers--United States. 3. Teachers--Training of--United
States. 4. Education--United States--Philosophy. I. Kysilka,
Marcella L.

LB1775.H68 1990   371.1'0023'73   90-4294
ISBN 0-912099-05-4

Published by Kappa Delta Pi
An International Honor Society in Education
P. O. Box A
West Lafayette, Indiana 47906

The purpose of Kappa Delta Pi is to recognize outstanding contributions to education. To this end it
invites to membership such persons who exhibit
commendable personal qualities, worthy educational
ideals, and sound scholarship, without regard to
race, color, religion, or sex.

Table of Contents

Becoming a Teacher

Final Thoughts

Prologue

During the 1986-88 biennium, I had the privilege of traveling about the United States, visiting schools and universities. This opportunity existed, partially, because of my role as President of Kappa Delta Pi. As I visited our schools and universities, I heard many of the same messages—the terrible plight of our schools and the frustrations felt by teachers, parents, students, university professors and other education professionals about what they could do to make things better. People in the field of education were angered, perplexed, astonished, and exasperated by the constant criticisms from various governmental agencies, the public, and yes, their own colleagues, about our public education. Often, the professional educators were trying to resolve conflicting demands made upon them by legislators and other influential bodies about how to improve education. On the one hand, schools were told to raise standards; on the other, they were reminded that they must provide equal educational opportunity for all students. Although these may not necessarily be opposing goals, the cry for immediate and sweeping action made them appear to be in direct conflict with one another.

The situation was exacerbated by the many national reform reports published during the 80s. Many of these reports were not written by well informed or well intentioned persons, but they became a focal point for the public's demand for improving our education system. No aspect of public education was spared. Our elementary schools failed because our students couldn't read, write or do arithmetic. Our secondary schools were failures because our students didn't measure up favorably to their foreign counterparts. Our universities were graduating mediocre products, students who could not function adequately in their chosen professions. And our teacher training institutions were abysmal failures. New teachers were a sad lot; they knew nothing about their content, and could not handle the problems existent in the public schools. The picture painted by the reform reports, the articles in the magazines read by the general public, and in the local newspapers was pretty grim. Yet those of us who have devoted many years of our professional lives to the field of education realized that the picture being painted was not necessarily the most accurate portrayal of American schools.

We have some superb schools in our country. They exist in large and small communities across this great country of ours. We, unlike most other countries of the world, have insisted that all of our children have a right to and free access to public education, throughout their lifetimes. We may not have been totally successful in carrying out our goals, but we keep working towards them—we believe in them. As a result, we have taken on numerous responsibilities within the public school structure that rightfully belong to other social and/or religious agencies. For example, sex education, drug abuse education, AIDS education, family counseling services, before and after school care for children, free breakfast and lunch programs, and the list goes on. Within these programs and within the "normal" curriculum of the school, we have some highly dedicated, talented, well-qualified, and absolutely excellent teachers who are frequently overlooked, overworked, and underpaid. These teachers work diligently to provide the best education possible for the children in their care and frequently are greeted with more criticism than praise.

There is no doubt that our schools and our teachers have an image problem with the public. We know about our failures and our successes, while the public is more aware of the failures rather than the successes. Because our schools are painted as bastions of failure, the public has little regard for the quality of our schools or for the people who devote their lives to the education of children. Questions such as, "Why do you want to teach?" or "You are so bright, why not do something more productive and rewarding than teaching?" are frequently thrust upon the "would-be" teacher. The problem, then, becomes, how can we as educators change this perception held by the public? How can we convince our constituencies that teaching is a terrific career—a most rewarding and influential profession? How can we convince the public that our schools are not fortresses of failure? How can we gain the respect we so rightfully deserve as teachers? How can we restore honor to the teaching profession?

These were the questions that we posed to the laureate members of Kappa Delta Pi. We asked these distinguished educators if they would take the time to reflect on the question of restoring honor to the teaching profession and to share with us, the educators of this country, their thoughts about what can and should be done to improve their image of teachers and schools.

The following essays are an interesting and divergent collection of thoughts and ideas. They fall into many categories. Some focus on the training of teachers; others deal with, as Alice Miel suggests, the celebration of teaching. Some of the authors remind us ever so diplomatically about our responsibilities as members of society to become involved in appropriate causes to improve the human condition. We are warned about the need for good role models for children, particularly for minority children. The debate is alive as to whether we are or are not a profession and whether we have had and lost, or never had "honor" as teachers.

I encourage you to read these essays carefully. There is much wisdom in these pages and we can learn from that wisdom. After I read these manuscripts, I was convinced, more than ever, that I chose the best "profession" for me. I know teachers are important.

I know teachers can make a difference. These teachers have, and they will continue to influence students for generations.

                                        Marcella L. Kysilka
                                        Past-President

Acknowledgements

This collection of thoughts, from some of education's greatest thinkers, could not have been assembled without the help of a number of people. First, the members of the Executive Councils of Kappa Delta Pi who conceptualized this project as a means of recognizing the thousands of teachers who diligently toil to provide good educational experiences and opportunities for our youth. These members include Bettye Caldwell, Louise Dieterle, Harold Drummond, Mark Hess, Bonnie Howard, Bruce Jorgensen, George Mehaffy, W. Ross Palmer, John Petry, Jennie Waters, and Rita Zerr.

Second, a great deal of thanks is given to the authors of the essays. As Past-President of Kappa Delta Pi, I contacted the already busy members of the Laureate Chapter of Kappa Delta Pi and asked them if they could find the time to write an essay on "Restoring Honor to the Teaching Profession." At the time of contact, I could only tell them that once the manuscripts were received and reviewed, we would decide if and how we would publish them.

Third, I need to thank William Alexander, Harold Drummond, Kaoru Yamamoto and Gerald Ponder, who helped to review the manuscripts and participated in the decision to publish them in this particular format.

Finally, a special note of thanks must be given to Gerald Ponder, who serves as Kappa Delta Pi's editor of monographs, and his assistant, Patricia Peters. They took care of all the technical aspects of publishing this monograph and made my job easy and enjoyable.

M. L. K.

A Message from the President

It is gratifying to have so many of our distinguished Kadelpians from the Laureate Chapter write on the theme "Restoring Honor to the Teaching Profession." It is not the theme but the Laureates' reflections on the theme which will enable us to think more clearly about honor in teaching.

Having participated in numerous Kappa Delta Pi meetings and conferences during my first year as president, it is clear that honor, dignity and respect in teaching is enormously important to beginning as well as experienced teachers. In an era of bad press, it is not surprising that many teachers question their value and importance as educators. Yet American teachers have much of which to be proud. For example, 84% of the inventions patented in the world are patented by Americans. Thirty-four percent of all academic Nobel prizes have been awarded to Americans. Who taught them and fostered this creativity?

My hope is that this anthology will serve as a springboard for discussions in colleges and universities, at KDP chapter meetings, and at professional conferences throughout the country. May these works contribute, in a significant way, to the validation of teaching as a noble and honorable profession.

Bruce Jorgensen

In Celebration of Teaching

Ernest Boyer, Alice Miel, and Ralph Tyler propose ways to look at what teachers have and can accomplish and what can be done by teachers, government agencies and the public to recognize the accomplishments of teachers.

Teaching in America

Ernest L. Boyer

The quality of education in this country can be no greater than the dignity we assign to teaching. And yet, teaching in this country remains an imperiled profession—not because salaries or credentialing standards are too low—but because day-to-day conditions in the schools leave many teachers more responsible but less empowered.

Since 1983, America has been engaged in the most sustained, bipartisan drive for school renewal in its history. Academic requirements have been tightened, standards have been raised, but most of the mandates for reform have been imposed top-down, and we're beginning to discover that outside regulation has its limits. Education is a human enterprise with teachers and students interacting with each other. There is just so much that can be accomplished by directives from above.

At the Carnegie Foundation, we recently surveyed thousands of teachers from coast-to-coast. We discovered that nearly one-third have no role in shaping the curriculum they are asked to teach; more than 50 percent do not participate in planning their own in-service education programs, and over 90 percent are not involved in selecting new teachers or administrators.

Teachers today are still faced with too many students, too much paperwork, too little time for preparation, and too many mindless interruptions. Moreover, teachers are not only called on to teach the "basics," they are also expected to monitor the playground, police for drugs, reduce teenage pregnancy and do what our homes, churches and communities have been unable to accomplish. And when teachers fall short anywhere along the line, we condemn them for not living up to our idealized expectations.

A classroom teacher responding to the Carnegie survey put the issue squarely:

> Education is the only profession out of which all others must grow. Yet it is the profession which gets the least recognition for its contributions to society. Perhaps more of the best and brightest would consider teaching as a career if it were accorded the professional status it deserves.

It's ironic that while industry now talks about involving plant workers in decisions, the school reform movements risks moving in just the opposite direction. A school, to flourish, must have an environment in which people work together. In such a setting, teachers stay in touch with current practices, and administrators involve teachers in school leadership. In the end, it is students who benefit when teachers are made full partners in the process.

Teachers also need a systematic program of renewal. In other professions—medicine and law, for example—such programs are assumed. Teacher recognition at the district level is required, and money should be available at the local school to support innovative ideas and make it possible for teachers occasionally to travel to professional meetings.

We need federal leadership as well. Thirty years ago, in response to Sputnik, President Dwight Eisenhower proposed the National Defense Education Act, a federally-funded teacher program that sent a powerful signal to the nation. Now we need a 1990 version of that initiative—a Teacher Excellence Act—that would, among other things, establish teacher institutes in every region of the country and provide fellowships to thousands of teachers from all fifty states, allowing them to spend time in libraries, in laboratories and with other teachers—the simple things that college professors just take for granted.

This act could also include a distinguished teaching fellows program in which master teachers in each state would spend a year moving from school to school, holding seminars with colleagues.

Recruiting better teachers is one of education's biggest challenges, and the federal scholarship program for gifted high school students who plan to enter teaching should be expanded. After all, we have a Peace Corps to send Americans overseas; why not attract the best and brightest to teach the rural poor and the disadvantaged in our inner cities here at home?

Indeed, the president should make teacher excellence a national crusade, and convene a dinner in the East Room of the White House for the fifty men and women designated by their states as teachers of the year. On this occasion, the president, as host, could affirm the dignity of teaching and invite the teachers to discuss the inspiration of their work. To heighten the impact of this event, it should be televised, prime time.

If we want better schools, this nation must find ways to identify great teachers and given them the recognition and opportunities for renewal they deserve. It's time to recognize that whatever is wrong with America's public schools cannot be fixed without the help of those already in the classroom. To talk about recruiting better students into teaching without examining the circumstances that discourage teachers is simply a diversion.

For half a decade, governors, legislators and corporate leaders have vigorously affirmed the essentialness of public education.

School renewal must build on this foundation. Excellence cannot be imposed from above. It can only be accomplished by inspired teachers who meet with children every day. The challenge now is to move beyond regulations, focus on renewal, and make teachers full participants in the process.

Bringing Honor to the Teaching Profession

Alice Miel

After accepting an invitation to contribute ideas on restoring honor to the teaching profession, I started searching for a way to approach the subject. Only when I began to question how we can *restore* something to the profession that it has never really possessed, did I find an entry to my part of this discussion. I found that I needed to substitute "bringing" for "restoring" honor in the charge.

A key concept I wish to elaborate in bringing honor to the teaching profession is *celebration*. Jean Betzner, in her teaching of elementary education at Teachers College, Columbia University in the forties and fifties, made much of celebration as a way of reaching and fortifying individual children. Celebrate birthdays, celebrate successes in learning something, celebrate accomplishments like pieces of writing, a drawing, a product of wood or clay, she would urge. "Accentuate the positive" was the underlying principle.

Celebration may be a private matter between student and teacher, as described by Susan OHanian in her article in the *Phi Delta Kappan.*[1] Leslie, a deaf child, had begun the year as a scared, spoiled, very demanding child. By February she had become so outgoing she had been able to sense her teacher's discomfiture during an "evaluation" visit by an authority figure. As Leslie left the classroom at the end of the day, she reassured the teacher with a hug and said, "Now don't worry. It's okay. You are doing a good job." And a note she left behind ended with a P.S.: "A lot of people love you."

Ask any teacher and you will learn that satisfaction with the job comes from a series of episodes which find the teacher and the taught celebrating together.

In addition, celebration often involves bringing someone to the attention of others so that a number can enjoy the achievement. Take, for example, the celebration described in my 1988 Christmas letter from a former student, a partially-sighted person who has done amazing things both before and after retirement.

"Last June at the graduate exercises of the private school in which I have done volunteer work for several years," she wrote, "I had a once-in-a-lifetime experience. A graduating eighth grader gave his speech and it was a tribute to me. I was so surprised! He never would have made it if it hadn't been for my help. Then he proceeded to give a blow by blow account of different things I had done for him.

"After the speech the headmaster rushed down and escorted me to the stage so everyone would know who I was. Afterward I received a tape of the whole program from a man who thought I should have it. Someone else sent me a photo of the little boy and me. The parents wrote a very thoughtful 'thank you.' I tell you this was a most moving and humbling experience. How could I ever really have meant all that?"

If the profession as a whole is to be held in honor, it is important that the participants in celebrations of teaching include an even wider public than parents in a particular school. It must have been rewarding for a high school history teacher in Chicago to receive newspaper recognition under the heading, "Quiet American Hero."[2] The report described how the teacher, every year since 1973, had led a band of teenagers, mostly black and Hispanic, to City Hall in a one-woman voter participation drive. It added to the value of the local publicity to have the article reprinted in a collection of newspaper clippings distributed throughout the nation by People for the American Way.

These few illustrations show what school officials and the public can find to celebrate if they take the advice of Susan OHanian to the new Secretary of Education to spend time finding out what really goes on in schools by visiting classrooms and talking with children, teachers and parents. There are enough instances of teaching worth celebrating to ensure that all teachers can experience the pleasure of having their work celebrated. While it may bring some honor to the profession to have awards given to "the teacher of the year," it could enhance good feelings about teachers if instances of celebration of teaching were to be multiplied by thousands. Public celebrations are important in part as mirrors in which teachers can see themselves as worthy.

Teachers themselves are responsible for creating something to celebrate by rising to their best. They should not hesitate to let others know of events in their teaching of which they are especially proud. An outstanding example of self reporting is Eliot Wigginton's account of twenty years of teaching in a high school classroom.[3] Teachers also can take leadership in calling attention to gifted work by colleagues, thus helping to build honor for their profession.

Because of modesty or unawareness of outstanding teaching actions, many occasions for celebration go unnoticed. Part of the difficulty in discovering reasons for celebrating teaching lies in the nature of teaching. A letter advertising the *Journal of Curriculum Theorizing* discusses this problem:

> Continuing debates concerning the characters and quality of teaching reveal the difficulty of describing teaching as a profession. It is portrayed as an art by those who want to maintain the autonomy of the teacher. It is defined as a science by those who prefer to analyze it, generalize it, predict and control it. We think it is interesting that this compulsion to capture teaching and pin it down is suffered by politicians, bureaucrats, scholars, administrators, everyone, it seems, but teachers.
>
> The editors of *JCT* are convinced that we and our colleagues have chosen to teach partly *because* teaching eludes simple and predictable descriptions. Whatever led us to this work initially, we remain teachers because teaching is interesting, complicated, perpetually and engagingly problematic.

Because teachers are in the thick of the action, they are in a good position to discern celebratable instances of teaching. They can be the first to discriminate between showy acting that leaves students in the shadow of the teacher and quiet leadership that helps students to flower.

Teachers will have the best opportunities to bring honor to themselves and their profession if they are treated as persons with insights and ideas that come from viewing the educative process from their vantage point. In school systems where teachers, parents, and administrators work together as a team, causes for celebration will extend beyond occasional laudatory bits of teaching to the joint efforts and successes of individual schools and school systems in providing superior education to the community. Honoring teaching could thus become commonplace.

Notes

[1]"A Not-So-Tearful Farewell to William Bennett," September, 1988, pp. 11-17.
[2]By Arthur J. Kropp, president of People for the American Way, in *The Kewanee Star-Courier*, July 10, 1988.
[3]*Sometimes a Shining Moment: The Foxfire Experience*. Garden City, NY: Anchor Press, 1985.

Placing Teaching in the Proper Perspective

Ralph W. Tyler

I believe that we are misled when we are told that the teaching profession has lost honor and it must be restored. I believe that our error is in failing to place teaching in the proper perspective. Teaching is not a stage production where an audience watches famous actors. Teaching is not a football game where the spectators cheer the successful plays of outstanding players. Teaching is more like parenting, in which each child is helped to develop into a constructive and happy person contributing to the continued development of a democratic society. Teaching is a personal service as well as a supremely social one.

All that separates people today from the savages of primitive society are the things people have learned. We are born with few, if any, characteristics different from primitive people, but beginning with birth, we are taught consciously or unconsciously to become more intelligent, more productive, more humane than the children in primitive societies. Without teachers we would still be in the Dark Ages. All the cultures of modern societies are built on education stimulated and guided by teachers. No other occupation is more important than teaching. The first step in gaining more public recognition of teaching is to explain and dramatize the great contribution to society that teaching makes. This can be done periodically at community meetings of civic clubs, religious gatherings, community improvement organizations and the like.

This continued reminder of the importance of teaching is essential to the development by the public of informed attitudes but it is not enough. Particular concrete illustrations are necessary to give real meaning to the general statement. This is the second step in gaining public recognition. In some schools in this large nation, there can always be found an outstanding example of a teacher's contribution. Recently, *The Reader's Digest* contained an article on the amazing success of a mathematics teacher in a high school in a depressed area of East Los Angeles. This teacher had more students passing the Advanced Placement Examination in mathematics than those in most high schools, even those in affluent suburbs. Reporting these outstanding examples in the national press two or three times a year in a press release that implies that such effective teaching can be found in many places in the nation is one way to clarify the meaning of good teaching.

A third step can be taken at the local level. Here the focus should be on the things being learned by local children under the guidance and stimulation of local teachers. At the high school level a number of achievements can be reported such as a student who never planned to go to college who was helped by his or her teacher to see the value of a college education and was encouraged by the teacher to set higher aspirations for education and career. Another illustration is students who became concerned about the air and water pollution in their community and, with the aid of their science teacher, measured different kinds of pollution. Then the students, with the aid of their English teacher, prepared a report on community pollution and, with the aid of their social studies teacher, met with several community groups to give them information to use in a determined effort to reduce community pollution. Or the biology class whose teacher helped the class establish a "laboratory" in a community child care center where they could learn how to provide for the physical, psychological and social needs of small children; in this way learning some of the things necessary to be good parents.

At the middle school level, other examples of the influence of good teachers can usually be found that are of interest to parents and other members of the community. For example, the sixth grade class whose teacher helped them to find out that there were residents of the local nursing home who were lonely and bored. These children took the responsibility to read stories to these older adults. Each afternoon three of the sixth graders went to the home and each child read to six adults. Or the fifth grade class, with the stimulation and aid of the teacher, who learned how to develop the family budget and then worked with the parents to produce a sound and balanced budget.

Even at the kindergarten level, the adults in the community can observe first hand the influence of a good teacher. Last month, I visited a primary school in western Massachusetts with a friend who lives in that community. We were greeted at the door by a child in the kindergarten who welcomed us in carefully pronounced English, and then introduced us to a third grade child who took us from room to room, introducing us to the teacher and the class. The teacher in each room then asked a child to explain what the class was doing and what they were learning. Then, at an assembly, I was asked to tell them about elementary schools in Ireland, since I had worked some summers at University College in Dublin.

These are only illustrations of the possibilities of presenting to the adult community actual samples of what teachers do and how they help the children and youth of the community to be constructive and responsible citizens. I believe that this direct presentation is far better than simply reporting test scores or athletic achievements. It should help the public to see that schooling is not a game where School X beat School B. Every school, with good teachers and concerned parents, can win the fight of education against ignorance.

Teaching is honored because it helps our children learn what is essential to successful and satisfying lives. It is done invisibly, often quietly. It is not a flashy performance on stage. It is the most honorable of the professions, and as it is understood by the public, it will be greatly honored.

A Call for Action

William Carr, Arthur Foshay, Harold Shane, and William Van Til express their thoughts on what teachers need to do to improve their image. Suggestions include the wise use of power; living an "educated life"; being an aware, futuristic, creative thinker; and realizing the important roles teachers can play as spokespersons and advocates for children and youth.

Counting the Spoons, or Restoring Honor to the Teaching Profession

William G. Carr

Honor for the teaching profession has clearly diminished lately. I will not agree that it has been irrevocably lost or totally destroyed.

Honor is a quality conferred by others. For teachers, as for other occupational groups, honor stems from public esteem. It is achieved by demonstration, not by a public announcement. It must be "earned the old-fashioned way" before it can be enjoyed. People extend honor because they find reason to believe it is deserved, not because they have heard it proclaimed.

Assertions of honor, if they are too importunate, may in fact provoke the reverse of the intended result. As Emerson said of a dubious and garrulous scoundrel, "The more he spoke of his honor, the faster we counted our spoons" (*Worship*, Harvard Classics edition, V:289).

Contributors to this series of articles are expected, no doubt, to suggest how teachers may increase the respect which the public extends to them. Let me begin with one step which will *not* in my opinion have a constructive effect. Teachers will not be honored because they reject or relinquish power.

True, teachers in recent years have become more powerful and less honored than before. But two simultaneous events are not always related as cause to effect.

"Power to the Teachers" has been, on the whole, a useful (and at times a necessary) slogan. In the future the power of teachers, both individually and through their organizations, is likely to be further augmented.

It is not power that corrupts its holders but the sordid and sinister purposes to which their power may be applied. Lord Acton to the contrary notwithstanding, power exerted for decent purposes is an ennobling, not a corruptive, influence. Indeed, the total absence of power may be an incitement to the worst depravity. The lady Isabella, in *Measure for Measure,* sums up the distinction memorably: "O, it is excellent to have a giant's strength; but it is tyrannous to use it like a giant" (Act III:2).

For centuries teachers, with few exceptions, lacked effective power to defend their own legitimate interests, let alone the rights of the students under their nominal control. In Colonial and early National America, for instance, indentured servants could be rented out by their owners as schoolmasters. A Philadelphia newspaper, as late as 1835, could publish the following notice describing one such servant as:

> . . . well-qualified for a clerk or to teach a school. He reads, writes, understands arithmetic, and accounts very well. Inquire of the Printer.

Although conditions have changed since then, during most of that long interval improvement was slow and small. Only in the last fifty years has the sluggish stream of teacher status quickened its pace.

Now it has plunged over its roaring Niagara, causing consternation among some spectators and carrying on its racing current a good deal of debris, some of it quite valuable.

This newly-acquired power of teachers may be used to elevate the quality of their public service or to decrease their burdens and increase their pay. The teachers themselves will have a hand in deciding how these purposes are balanced.

I believe the recent history of our profession is essentially the record of a continual struggle in the minds of teachers to determine how new power shall serve them.

I am no longer in a position to influence the outcome of that struggle or even to estimate the direction in which the balance is moving. In my opinion, however, the more the profession advertises its honor, the more carefully a skeptical public will count its spoons. When the public notices the rising quality of service, the public acclaim and the honor afforded will ensue.

Decisions about the uses of power will be made by individual teachers and their organizations. But since organizations depend in the last analysis on the steadfast and willing support of their members, the decision ultimately falls to the individual. Teachers themselves must decide what uses of power will give them the greatest and most enduring satisfaction. And what do teachers want most earnestly? Is it more leisure? More income? Success for their students? Public respect? Self respect?

It is easy to deceive oneself and others in responding to such questions. Nonetheless, people who have come into power must answer them. Even a refusal to confront the issue constitutes a kind of answer by default. It seems to me that teachers' organizations would serve their members better in this respect if their policies were more concentrated and therefore more easily evaluated by their members. A teachers' organization does not increase its usefulness by becoming a political party in disguise.

Professional teachers' organizations will attract more public esteem for their members if they attend to those issues on which teachers possess special competence, skill, information, and insight. An organization embroiled in every issue of broad social policy suffers at least two disadvantages. Neither of them is likely to increase public esteem. First, the organization is enfeebled by disunity. Second, the effort to be all things to all members weakens attention to those educational problems on which the public most needs the informed advice of its teachers.

Meanwhile, individual teachers, like other citizens, retain their inalienable right to take personal decisions on any political or social issue and to work with other individual citizens of like mind.

Two other fairly common maladies threaten the teaching profession and impair public esteem for professional opinion. Let us call them Aristophobia and Neophilia. Victims of the former develop an unreasonable fear of excellence. In advanced cases they may actually hate the very thought of distinctions of any kind. The once-respectable word "elite" may go quite out of style and become a term of reproach. Pressures are developed to minimize or ban examinations of both students and teachers and to avoid all comparisons of one person with another.

Neophiliacs suffer from another disease. They exalt novelty into a cult. Victims convince themselves that things are always better when they change. Educational procedures are applauded if they "excite" students rather than make them better or wiser or—more modestly—well-informed.

Something has happened lately to disturb public confidence in teachers and their organizations. If they want to regain, retain, and enhance public esteem, teachers should act so as to show the public that they desire, *above all else*, the best possible education for their children and youth. The task is as disarmingly simple and as desperately difficult as that. Of course, if this goal is not the truth, if the real concern of teachers is elsewhere, public confidence will not be augmented. Then, no matter what public relations devices are employed, honor will not come to teaching.

The determining decision in the next few years will be, I think, to define our true priorities. I hope and trust that this process is now underway and that it will be expedited. In that event, every assembly of teachers might become, like Kappa Delta Pi itself, "an International Honor Society."

Let's Teach!

Arthur W. Foshay

Teaching has always been an honorable profession. The greatest leaders in our philosophic, religious, cultural, scientific, and political traditions have all been teachers. We who have devoted our lives to this calling have as our heritage a line of prophets and servants of mankind who have given us knowledge, skill, and wisdom. They, and we in their likeness, help others toward self-realization. That's who we are. This may sound pretentious, but it is the simple truth, and everyone knows it.

Why, then, do we speak of *restoring* honor to teaching? The problem is that, especially in the United States, the honor of teaching exists but is not publicly recognized. There is something we can do about it.

We can demonstrate to the public what good teaching is, and what teachers wish for the community. Some of us have lost our idealism, but we can restore it by making known what we stand for. There are several ways open to us. I shall discuss some of them here.

Let us begin by agreeing on what an education is. Education broadens the awareness of people, hence their ability to be discriminating and to make sound judgments. This can be done systematically, through organized instruction, but not all of it need take place in schools. It can also take place in the workplace, in the community, through the media, and at home. One thing we teachers can do is to call attention to the opportunities to increase one's education in these other settings. We can lead the community to become educative in this sense.

We know something about the forms of knowledge that most people don't know. The function of the arts, for example, is to make available aspects of human experience not otherwise available, and thus to broaden one's awareness. Serious paintings offer the possibility of learning to see skillfully. Community leaders can learn to see the downtown area the way an artist would, and thus to improve the quality of their plans for civic development. People can learn to hear with skill, and the quality of publicly available music will improve because an audience will have been created. People can learn to move with skill, and the community will support dance as well as athletics. Again, we who have taught science know that it is much more than the gathering of facts. Objects of scientific interest are much more than curiosities. That's why the local museum is an important source of scientific understanding—an awareness that has become urgent in our time.

These possibilities and many others like them exist, but they cannot be brought to reality without teaching. We teachers can help other people to learn. That is our function in the world. However, teaching requires specialized knowledge. We have it, and most people don't. We, for example, know the difference between teaching and telling. We know what is implied by the phrase, "you learn what you do." You don't learn what is presented to you; you learn your response to what is presented. We know how to turn what otherwise would be random experience into learning experience. Whatever the question or problem, we know how it can be expressed clearly. We know how essential entertainment is, but we never confuse it with education.

We can show people how to add purpose to living in many areas of life, and in many settings.

The point is that teachers have specialized knowledge about teaching and learning. The public doesn't know this. Most people believe that all that is required of a teacher is knowledge of the subject matter. We know much better. We have seen too many experts in the content who cannot teach. The world is full of people who can do, but can't teach. We can.

What all this means is that we can gain the recognition we need by showing our specialized skills and knowledge where they will do the community some good. We can be the people who, in public affairs, offer advice about how to turn apathy into participation, how to offer information to the public in ways that promote positive action, how to make our communities educative in the important sense.

I learned this from a great educator, Harry Study (pronounced with a long u), who was superintendent of schools in Springfield, Missouri, many years ago. Mr. Study never stopped teaching and learning. He ate lunch at the local railroad station restaurant, where he was available for informal conversation with anyone. People sought him out there. He taught an Adult Sunday School class, and he frequently taught the children in the schools. He constantly conferred with the business and civic leaders of the town, and taught them about the possibility of education of good quality both in the schools and in the broader community. When Leonard Rose, the famous cellist, came to town, Study was there for the concert and didn't fail to call attention to the fact that it took place in the high school auditorium, where the local city orchestra performed frequently. He taught and learned while conferring with the school staff. He taught parents, and anyone (like me) who came along. He personally exemplified the well-educated, endlessly curious man. Mr. Study knew exactly who he was, and what he was doing. He was a teacher, and he taught. Appropriately, a school was named after him because he reminded his community of the honor of teaching.

There is, of course, much more that might be said about the kinds of education we would like to foster in the community. We would like families to confer about the choice of TV programs. We would like it if parents would ask their children to teach them what they had learned in school, day by day. We would like to participate in the improvement of community problem-solving. Working through others, we would like to have a constructive influence on our communities.

But can we? Two requirements have to be met. One is that we make room for this kind of community activity without sacrificing our personal lives to it, and the other is that we act with skill when we present ourselves publicly.

Concerning finding room: since the way we spend our time expresses our priorities, and our priorities arise from our values, we begin by considering what we value. I suggest here that we take ourselves with utter seriousness. Each of us has chosen the life we live. In addition to our classroom work, we have private lives. In deciding how to spend our time and energy, it is proposed here that each of us acknowledge the basic importance to us and others of our commitment to teaching. When we do, our public and private lives nourish one another, and we will find room for both. The problem is one of attitude before it is one of practicality. Shift the attitude, and the practical problems can be sorted out and given their proper place.

There are skills to be brought into play when working with the community. One of them has to do with how the public is to view us. As things stand, we speak to the public about the needs we have in the schools: smaller classes, better materials, better working conditions and salaries. Important as these matters are, if they are the whole content of our message to the community, we are viewed as a burden, a problem, clearly not as an asset. It follows that our professional organizations should improve the message they send out, and that we should too, personally.

Physicians do this successfully. We could learn from them. Physicians spend most of their effort informing the public about what is good for people. They have learned to keep the message positive and simple: what, specifically, to do and what to avoid. A good example of this is their message about nutrition: eat the "basic seven" food groups, in moderation, every day.

Let's consider an educational "basic seven." Here's an example.

To improve your education, that is, to broaden your awareness, do the following at least once each week:

1. *Read at least one serious magazine article, and talk it over at home.*
2. *Take part in one ambitious cultural activity, and talk it over.*
3. *Do something creative—make something of your own.*
4. *Survey the reading material in the house, to keep it well balanced between periodicals and books, and between "light" and "serious" material.*
5. *Have a family conference on what TV programs to let in.*
6. *Ask the children to teach the family what they have learned in school. (Don't ask them what happened at school. They will always say "nothing," meaning "nothing unusual.")*
7. *Stop in at the public library or a book store. Browse.*

There are other skills to be used. One of them is to help the local newspaper editor to find significant educational news—not just sentimental human interest stories or complaints. If the class is going on an excursion, let the paper and the other media know about it. Invite prominent local people to participate in a school event, and while they are there, ask them to talk with the students and respond to their comments and questions. Let the local editor know about it. Letters to the editor make a difference. Teachers aren't used to thinking of themselves as newsworthy, but they are. The point is this: if the local media editors haven't heard about it, they can't report it. If they don't report it, people don't know enough about us to honor what we do.

We could follow Harry Study's example. Let's face the public with our attention on the main thing—the possibility of a good education as a way of living a life. We can help all kinds of people to increase their awareness of themselves and what is around them, and thus to be discriminating and to make sound judgments. Let's teach. That is where our honor—and eventually our well-being—lies.

Creating Professionalism Which Commands Respect

Harold G. Shane

At least since 1893, when the NEA's Committee of Ten made its report,[1] both individuals and groups have written at length about ways to restore honor to the teaching profession.[2] As used in this essay the term refers to restoring a high public regard for the profession and the individual educator's integrity.

Long reports and entire volumes have been published on the topic of improving teaching and learning. A widely publicized example is *A Nation at Risk,* which was published by the National Committee on Excellence in Education in 1983. It was followed by a flood of analogous reports and proposals after it appeared.

Our emphasis here is on what may well prove to be two of the most important strategies to be employed in creating professionalism which commands respect. One of these is "educated hindsight," the other is "anticipatory foresight" in curriculum planning.

Educated hindsight. It is important for educators to look in their "rear vision mirrors," to scan the past and learn what we can do to update and, if appropriate, to implement an abundance of good ideas and innovations from earlier in the 20th century. A few illustrations are in order:

1901	Flora J. Cooke, as Director of the Francis W. Parker School, emphasized the importance of motivating learners and created the curriculum approach that later became known as the "project method."
1904	J.L. Meriam, at the University of Missouri Elementary School, introduced large blocks of time to replace conventional subject matter periods.
1908	William A. Wirt in Gary, Indiana, devised the platoon grouping system.
1914	Caroline Pratt established the importance of play in children's learning.
1917	The Lincoln School at Teachers College, Columbia University, pioneered experimental and scientific curriculum units in grades 1-6.
1919	Superintendent of Schools Carleton W. Washburne conceived the "Winnetha Plan," which provided for teaching in terms of individual difference.

| 1920 | Individual differences, particularly for the handicapped, also were stressed in the Dalton School Laboratory Plan. |

| 1923 | Cooperative curriculum planning was pioneered by Franklin Bobbitt in the Los Angeles Public Schools. |

| 1935-1942 | The Eight-year Study was developed and, after years of research, publicized progressive curriculum practices under Progressive Education Association sponsorship and with scholarly direction from such leaders as Ralph Tyler. |

And so on . . .

In addition to rediscovering and utilizing appropriate professional information from the past there is a need—perhaps an even greater need—to explore the implications of the impact which our germinating technosocial changes are having on our global environment and on the community-and-home milieu. This brings us to some of the ways in which "anticipatory foresight" can raise the profession to even more honored levels.

Developing "anticipatory foresight." The foresight involved here is an extension of the educational version many teachers and administrators have of what a curriculum for the 1990's should include with respect to both traditional subject matter content and methods to be used in the classroom.

Anticipatory foresight, as previously defined by the writer,[3] refers to the individual educator's ability to grasp the seismic confrontations we are having with rapidly accruing technosocial changes. We must also recognize that massive innovations in classroom practice and curriculum content must be made in the context of what is happening to the home and to the community of which they are an integral part.

To achieve the foresight needed to anticipate educational futures in the 1990's and beyond, educators need to invest more of their time and energy in significant reading and research; less on TV programs and purely entertaining books and magazines.

The many problems which must be tackled as we work to increase the honor in which an informed profession should be held, as implied early, can be inventoried in two categories: (1) National and global, along with (2) Home and community.

What must we learn about such items as the following? Also, what are the efficacious solutions to be sought, and how shall we introduce learners in all age groups, at appropriate levels of maturity, to the behaviors humans must acquire if they are to strive successfully to keep their planet safe and supportive?

- **The population crisis.** Since 1974 the world's population has increased by one billion. By 1988 there were over five billion inhabitants, and 10 billion humans could inhabit our planet in an early decade of the coming millennium.

- **Too many dollars; too little sense?** America and Americans are deeply in debt. A national, perhaps a global financial crisis is quite likely in the near future. As of 1988 the U.S. government was over $2 trillion in debt, corporations owed about the same, and individuals owed approximately $2.3 trillion. Our debt dollars apparently greatly exceed our sense!

- **The trend toward crowded "megacities."** The World Future Society estimates by the year 2000 over 50% of earth's inhabitants will live in massive communities. Projection of current trends suggests that huge urban units may well house 90% of the population by 2100. The status of transportation, schooling, public safety, and many similar elements will require careful thought and action.
- **The aging of Americans.** By 1988 over 8% of Americans were over 65. In 20 to 30 years, if trends continue, perhaps one fifth of our citizens will be over 65! How pension and health care costs can be borne are matters which demand the wisdom of careful future planning by our children and ourselves.

At least several dozen challenges such as the samples given require foresight and continuing self-education by educators as they contemplate the kinds of intellectual input that present and coming generations must experience.

Hunger, the AIDS epidemic, various nuclear dangers, pollution, working mothers (one-third of which have children aged five years or younger), child care crises, 287 youth gang homicides during 1987 in *just one* large city in the U.S., drug abuse, and 1988 Census Bureau data indicating that 30% of American children are born of unwed mothers (most of them teenage girls) constitute a further overview of some of the problems that must be faced.

Finding solutions to our dilemmas and challenges will restore not only the respect and integrity of the teaching profession. Sound solutions are a prerequisite to the restoration of our *national* honor!

Yesterday's curricula must be examined with a foresight that anticipates not only conventional skills in language, science, mathematics and the like. The curricula of the 1990's must reflect what our youth must learn as they face and overcome the new, contemporary problem-oriented demands which have surfaced in such alarming numbers.

In fine, honor can and must be restored to our profession—but only as an integral part of restoring the concomitant national integrity which has carried the American Dream toward fulfillment in years gone by.

Notes

[1] National Education Association, *Report of the Committee of Ten on Secondary School Studies*. New York: American Book Company, 1894.

[2] The term **honor,** as a noun and as a verb, has a dozen or more definitions in an unabridged dictionary. Among them are high regard, good reputation, integrity, a sense of right and wrong, and adherence to principles deemed to be right.

[3] cf. Harold G. Shane, "Educational Foresight as an Essential Element in the Computerized World of 1990-2040," *Computerworld*, (Special 1000th Issue of the journal), 3 November, 1986.

Restoring Honor to the Teaching Profession: A Call for Action

William Van Til

Restore honor to the teaching profession? Surely this is not needed. For the dictionary tells us that honor means integrity, honesty, probity, and respect for what is right. The typical member of the teaching profession possesses these characteristics in abundance; unlike business, government and the media, the teaching profession, though otherwise often criticized, is not under fire for lacking honor. If honor is missing in our society we must look elsewhere than to the teaching profession. Look elsewhere for greed, insider trading, shady deals, blindness to environmental pollution; look elsewhere for sleaze, corruption, lying by officials, negative mudslinging campaigns; look elsewhere for trash TV, for pornography in advertisements, and for the exaltation of celebrities who behave grossly and receive enormous financial rewards. There is no necessity to restore honor to an already honorable profession.

So what must be meant by "restoring honor to the teaching profession"? Another usage of the word "honor" must be intended—esteem, respect, admiration on the part of the public. But the implication of the word "restoring" is that the American public once held education in honor but now no longer does. "Restoring" apparently means that we must return to some vanished golden era when the teaching profession was highly esteemed, respected, and admired by the general public. But the "good old days" of a teaching profession held in honor by the citizenry never existed, as teachers from the time of Ichabod Crane to the present could testify. The teacher in America has usually been portrayed to the public as futile, or comic, or confused, or ineffectual, or all four. As to monetary rewards, the American teacher has always been low person on the professional totem pole.

That the teaching profession is not highly esteemed, respected, and admired today by the American citizenry is apparent. Yes, there are verbal affirmations of honor by campaigning politicians, and occasional lip worship by committees of business leaders advocating school reforms linked to corporate profitability, as well as honest tributes by honest people. But the test of words is action. The reality is that teachers today are an underpaid group, usually ill-equipped with materials of instruction, often working in surroundings that defeat them, and uninvolved in planning the broad educational program.

What can educators do about the lack of honor accorded the teaching profession? We could, of course, follow the example of Shakespeare's King Richard III, who cried, "Let us sit upon the ground and tell sad stories of the death of kings." But this, however consoling, does nothing to change the situation. Nor will superficial solutions, such as a teacher in space or merit pay or awards for excellence, make any real difference.

Major changes on four fronts must occur if the teaching profession is to be held in honor in American life. 1) We will need to put our own house in order. 2) We will need to reeducate the public as to the true curriculum fundamentals. 3) We will need to dedicate ourselves to a wider conception of the well-being of children and youth. 4) We will need to work with like-minded citizens to achieve a better society. Let us consider each of these formidable fronts.

If we are to achieve improvements within our own house, we teachers need as a profession to have a greater say in our own affairs. More say as to materials and curriculum; more say too as to administration and management. If we have learned anything from studies of curriculum development and supervision it is that for school improvement to come about we need expanded teacher participation in planning and implementation. All school conditions that give teachers opportunities to be creative, innovating, and experimental should be supported by the profession; all conditions that reduce teachers to mechanical followers of formulas should be opposed. What makes a professional? Expertness, competence, skill and experience are words descriptive of the professional. Until the public sees such words as applicable to teachers we have little chance to be regarded as a profession comparable to those of the doctors and lawyers. Puppets are not professionals. Full participation in the total conduct of profession is the mark of the professional.

If education is to be honored, it is time for educators to be heard on curriculum. Too long the debate on education has been dominated by policy makers outside the educational community. Take the reform reports of the 1980's, for instance. During the past decade there has been little input by educators into national reports. John Goodlad's and Ernest Boyer's reports are among the honorable exceptions. Though both excellence and equality should characterize American schools, many of the reform reports of the 1980's focused on achieving excellence and rendered only lip service to achieving equal educational opportunity in American life for Blacks, Hispanics and children of the poor. Proposals for improving the learning of the 3 R's often did not recognize the central importance of meaningful content and the power of the family environment. Reports such as *A Nation at Risk* singled out, from among the many possible goals for American education, economic competition against societies such as Japan's; other goals for education were minimized.

Reform reports have often recommended more of the same—more of the content and methods that haven't worked well before, more required courses, more credits for graduation, more remedial work to teach what hasn't been learned because of its meaninglessness. Legislators have responded by joining the numbers game—more graduation requirements, longer school years, more time on task. (The use of the word "task" is a characteristic misconception of the proper relationship of teachers and students in the educational enterprise.) The eighties were the decade in which more of what wasn't succeeding was mistaken for improvement.

The time has come to turn away from quack remedies and to speak up for the authentic fundamentals of curriculum development. Put most plainly, American educators should meet the needs of children and youth, help them to understand and act on imperative social realities of their time, and teach them to live a democratic way of life. Fundamentally we educate in the 3 R's, in the curriculum fields, and in interdisciplinary studies in order to meet needs, cope with social realities, and form humane values.

Educators should speak up for an education which meets the real personal and social needs of children and youth. For psychology has taught us that unless learners see connections between what is to be learned and the individual's experience there is little learning. When students are concerned, involved, excited, centered on problems real to them, they learn. When the content taught is sterile and meaningless and unrelated to their experiences, the result of teaching is, as George Santayana has pointed out, the acquisition of inert knowledge, swiftly forgotten. "We learn what we live," wrote William Heard Kilpatrick.

Educators should speak up for education in social realities. Young people live with us in a world that presents perplexing social problems and difficult choices. Society daily affects the quality of their lives. Young people are tomorrow's citizens, employed people, family members, and social problem solvers. Good teachers in many curricular fields can relate social realities to the learner's world. We can educate for social responsibility while meeting the needs of the young.

Another curriculum fundamental is value formation. We must educate for a way of life characterized by the use of intelligence, respect for the individual, and commitment to human welfare. This way is spelled out in the documents of democracy. It is supported by the basic values of world religions and the findings of scientific inquiry. The values of a democratic way of life must be learned anew by each generation and applied to a changing world. Yesterday's threat to democracy took the form of totalitarianism. Today's threat is more subtle. It takes the form of apathy and ignorance. Benjamin Franklin foresaw it in his answer to a question as he left the Constitutional Convention, "What have we got, a republic or a monarchy?" Franklin responded, "A republic, if you can keep it." Thomas Jefferson wrote, "If a nation expects to be ignorant and free, it expects what never was and never will be."

If the public is to respect education as a profession, the public must hear educators on the goals and methods and content of schooling. The field cannot be ceded to politicians and businessmen, though they too should be heard. This is our profession; we should be heard on schooling. Educational leaders should be heard through writing for the lay public and through radio and TV appearances. Educational organizations should be heard through resolutions and releases by presidents, boards, executive secretaries. Educators at the grass roots should be heard through contributions to school board meetings, letters to the editor, cooperation with local broadcasters, meetings with parents.

Nor should educators limit themselves to matters of philosophy and curriculum within the schools. They should play an active role as advocates of better lives for children and youth. If education is to be honored as a profession, we must dedicate ourselves to a wider conception of the well-being of children and youth. Who else is there who can better represent children and youth? Children and youth are our constituency. Who is as well qualified to speak on behalf of their education, health, living conditions, and societal well-being? Unlike other professions we live every working day with children and youth; we know them as does no other profession.

Advocacy for children and youth is especially needed right now. We must become advocates for the young to compensate for the decline in caring in our society. In the 80's the number of children growing up in poverty increased; today more than one child in five is born poor. One half of all Black children under six live in poverty as do 40% of Hispanics under 18. The young are a growing percentage of the homeless. Three out of ten American children are born out of wedlock. Drug use has risen shockingly among children as well as youth. Conditions in and around many inner city schools are chaotic. Yet federal programs on behalf of children and youth have been sharply curtailed. State and local governments have been unable or unwilling to provide enough needed help. Problems of the young with respect to education, health, nutrition, recreation have become formidable. A new generations of youngsters has become the victim of society's neglect.

Ernest Boyer, president of the Carnegie Foundation for the Advancement of Teaching, states in the foreword of his report, *The Condition of Teaching*, "Large majorities of teachers find poverty, poor health, undernourishment, and neglect to be problems at their schools." Teachers from every state were canvassed in twin surveys conducted by mail in the spring and fall of 1987. Among the findings:

- 90 percent said lack of parental support was a problem at their schools.
- 89 percent said there were abused or neglected children at their schools.
- 69 percent said poor health was a problem for their children.
- 68 percent said some children were undernourished.

"Teachers repeatedly made the point that in the push for better schools they cannot do the job alone," said Boyer.

Not for ourselves but for children and youth we educators should urge a Marshall Plan for the reconstruction and staffing of inner city schools. Not for ourselves but for them we should advocate pre-schooling. Not for ourselves but for them we should urge full funding of Headstart which now reaches only 20% of the eligible children. Not for ourselves but for them we should call for investment in elementary and secondary education in the form of materials, salaries, and buildings in which education has a chance to prevail. Not for ourselves but for them we should work to foster literacy, develop analytical thinking skills, and reduce dropouts. Not for ourselves but for them we should support opportunities for higher education for those who need scholarships, loans, and work. Not for ourselves but for them we should foster programs of teacher education that combine liberal education with theory and practice in teaching programs.

Our advocacy for the young must go beyond support for education. We should be vigorous in support of family issues such as care during pregnancy, parental leave, nutrition programs, child day care programs, programs to aid homeless children. We should support health programs, recreational facilities, and decent housing for young people. For our proper role is to be spokespeople on behalf of the unrepresented young.

The 1988 presidential campaign demonstrated the necessity for strong advocacy of the welfare of the young by our profession. Despite claiming that he aspired to be the "education president" and despite surrounding himself with children in commercials, George Bush seldom discussed education and its problems, save for a merit schools program for disadvantaged schools and wider establishment of magnet schools. Michael Dukakis limited himself largely to proposing wider opportunities for college attendance. Symbols such as the pledge of allegiance, the murderer Willie Horton, and mandated public school prayer dominated the campaign. Specific proposals for action on the pressing problems of American education were few. The campaign disappointed and discouraged educators.

Yet we do have potential allies in the struggle on behalf of the young. The citizenry supports programs in the interest of children and youth. Though the teaching profession may not be held in honor, the American people want the best possible lives for their children. Surveys have shown that, by three to one, the American people support full funding of health and education programs despite the federal deficit. Though elementary and secondary school students are politically voiceless, their parents and grandparents are not and would support our advocacy. With enough pressure from the grass roots, political establishments must respond.

Yes, critics will say that because of the federal deficit and financial stringency at the state and local levels there is not money available for programs on behalf of young Americans. In response we should point out that America's priorities in the 1980's as to spending are distorted. Immediately after the 1988 elections, the site of a supercollider program to cost 4.4 billion was announced; operating costs over the next 25 years are estimated at more than 11 billion. The General Accounting Office estimates the cost of cleaning up toxic waste at 130 billion. Billions are proposed for the Strategic Defense Initiative, familiarly called Star Wars. Shaky and badly managed savings and loan institutions are being bailed out at a cost estimated at 136 billion in 1988, and growing by billions with new 1989 figures.

In contrast to these **billions**, the current administration in Washington talks in terms of **millions** for education. Five hundred million are proposed for merit schools and 50 million proposed for magnet schools. May I remind you that it takes one thousand million to take one billion? May I remind you that Michael Milken, the alleged swindler, had an income of 550 million dollars in one year from his Wall Street deals? That this is more than President Bush's proposal for funding merit school programs for the disadvantaged? Our priorities are askew. **Billions** are proposed for a supercollider, for Star Wars, for toxic waste cleanup, for the military establishment, for shaky savings and loan institutions. Yet, when we ask for funding for education, we are told that money is tight and that the nation cannot finance badly needed education programs. If our federal government was able to finance a moon landing, we should be able to provide better lives for young Americans on earth. If state and local governments can give Japanese industrialists financial incentives to locate in their areas, we should be able to finance nutrition, health and education for a new generation of Americans.

The most frightening deficit in America is not the federal deficit. It is the deficit in providing for the education and well-being of the young. Let us hold President George Bush to his repeated commitment to a "kinder, gentler nation." Let us hold the Congress, which is controlled by the Democratic Party, to the support of educational and health improvements that the members have promised. The people want federal deficit reduction but not at the expense of the most vulnerable Americans, the young. The people know that the most needed investment of all is in their children. If educators rise to the challenge individually, through all of their organizations, and in alliance with citizens, the voice of the people can be heard. And in the process, as a by-product, respect for education as a profession will grow.

There is also a fourth front to work on, if we are to be respected as professionals. While being active advocates who *lead* in the struggle for better lives for children and youth, educators also can continue to work as citizens for a better society for Americans of all ages and a better world for all inhabitants of this planet. Organizations worthy of our support already exist; they need our participation as fellow citizens in improving the environment, supporting arms control, and reducing the gap between haves and have-nots, to cite only a few imperative problems. Many foot soldiers, including educators, are needed in such causes and movements working for a better society. Identification with voluntary organizations of our individual choice, including political parties, provides us still more arenas as citizens. Working with our fellow citizens for a better society and world can lead to greater respect for educators as members of a profession concerned for all human beings.

So what must be done if the teaching profession is to be regarded with honor by the public? There are no easy paths, only difficult roads. We have suggested: 1) getting our own house in order through full participation, 2) speaking out on needed curriculum improvements, 3) becoming active advocates for the well-being of children and youth, 4) joining fellow citizens as co-workers for a better society and world. If we fill such roles, we will not only win respect and be honored as a profession by the public but will also achieve self-respect and an inner sense of our own worth.

Becoming a Teacher

This collection of essays by Robert Anderson, Harry Broudy, Elliot Eisner and Ned Flanders focuses on becoming a teacher. The importance of appropriate education, a body of common knowledge, a balance of theory and practice, attention to both the science and art of teaching are addressed in these essays.

Works in Progress

Robert H. Anderson

While it would be reckless to assert that all of us who became Kappa Delta Pi laureates were great teachers during our service in public school classrooms, it may be reasonable to assert that we found pleasure and satisfaction in such work, to the point that we have dedicated the rest of our lives to the study and the exaltation of classroom service. An opportunity to honor the teaching profession in this special publication is therefore a welcome one.

Among my favorite magazines is *The Sciences*, one of whose regular departments is devoted to reports on unfinished but fascinating activities/inquiries/projects in which various individuals or groups of scientists are engaged. These essays, written by Russ Rymer, invariably reveal that a great deal has already been learned, developed, or discovered about the topic or problem in question, but they also offer piquant insight into the continuing mysteries and the challenging questions that remain to be probed. The apt title for this series is "Works in Progress," a not-uncommon phrase that has been given rich meaning for me through Rymer's artful mixture of praise for enterprising people and already-earned knowledge, and suspenseful anticipation of even greater wisdom. I have decided to steal the title for this, my own essay in celebration of teachers, to convey the notion that good teachers, too, are "works in progress" whose present status is praiseworthy but whose future discoveries and accomplishments are even more to be valued.

My central thesis is that teaching is as complex and challenging as any professional role in our society. This is contrary to the prevailing public and legislative view of teaching, which is defined as relatively simple work if only one "knows his stuff" and is sufficiently diligent about managing the process. One need only examine the difference between the advance preparation that by law and custom is provided in universities and in other contexts (e.g., hospitals and legal offices) for other professionals, and the very thin requirements and arrangements that prevail for preparing teachers. Further, there are sharp contrasts between the working conditions, supervisory services, and opportunities for further professional learning that obtain in education, and those that prevail in other fields. One explanation for these discrepancies is that the general public, through elected officials, controls entry regulations and budgetary decisions, whereas most other professionals are in a position to control their own entry and working conditions, including fees and charges. A taxpayer can't do much but grumble if legal or hospital costs seem too high, but he/she can in fact keep the education budget at a low level.

Anyone who has ever visited a physician's or a dentist's office, or even looked at the walls of an automobile dealer's service area, is aware of numerous framed certificates that testify to time and energy spent successfully in a re-training or updating program that makes it safer (than before) to bring in one's teeth or bones or Chevrolet for servicing. But look in vain in school corridors for certificates that pronounce a recent significant investment in the teachers' repertoires that makes it safer (than before) to bring in children's brains, personalities, and emotional apparati for daily maintenance.

Reluctance on the part of the general public to invest in greater competence derives less from a malevolent posture, although former Education Secretary Bennett's hostile pronouncements seemed to enjoy public support, but rather from a naive view of what schools and teaching are all about. That view is gradually changing, but certification requirements and working conditions are not likely to change dramatically in our lifetime. Therefore, beginning teachers will probably continue to launch their careers with much-less-than-sufficient training, and teachers in service will probably continue to receive much less help and resources than would make sense if our society really wanted to educate its young at a state-of-the-art level. So be it: but thanks, praise, and godspeed to those dedicated people who strive nonetheless to perform at a high level and to learn as much as possible about the nurturance of learning.

And oh, there is now so much to learn! Teachers live in one of the most dynamic periods in history, and knowledge about human growth and development and about efficacious learning environments is literally exploding. That the knowledge is not well organized and packaged, and often tentative and confusing, makes it difficult to absorb and apply. Furthermore, the scholars are, as indeed they should be, in energetic disarray, so that classroom teachers have to figure out most things for themselves.

Which brings me to a major proposition. "By themselves," I strongly believe, must mean not one-at-a-time, but in a collective effort. This essay is not the place to argue once again the debilitating effects upon teachers of working alone in self-contained classrooms, but it is a place to argue that one's professional education must involve intense and continuing interaction with others. Such interaction is almost inescapable within the teaching team; but other forms of collegiality are available, and teachers should welcome all such opportunities.

Shoshana Zuboff, author of *The Age of the Smart Machine*, tells in an interview (see Emmons, 1988) about a very advanced manufacturing operation whose manager, noting the extent of company investment in the ongoing intellectual development of the employees, was toying with the idea of calling the plant a college. More and more of what workers were doing from day to day, she observed, was some form of learning, based on their engagement with abstract information and figuring out new courses of action based on what they had learned. Further, Zuboff notes, "work and learning had become increasingly interconnected, and the organization had to become a learning environment if the work was to be carried out optimally." She concludes that "collegiality, rather than functional differentiation, will mark the future workplace."

Work in progress, in other words, is both the activity and the thinking/reflection/inventiveness of the people engaged in it. The worker is a potential masterpiece, and each new skill or insight or talent brings that worker's performance closer to an ideal. Support, encouragement, recognition, and reward on the part of colleagues and the managers of the work environment lead to further effort in the direction of that ideal. In the absence of interaction to prompt such effort, the striving is less likely to persist.

Donald A. Schon made an important contribution to our thinking about collegial interaction through his 1983 book, *The Reflective Practitioner*. Following discussion of the usual working conditions and the teacher isolation that prevails within the educational bureaucracy, Schon observes that such an environment tends to discourage reflection-in-action. Teachers, he states, have a strong need to communicate their private puzzles and insights and test them against the views of peers (p. 333). Other scholars share this view, and propose in addition that adult learning is essentially a social activity.

Not only learning for its own sake, but other advantages derive from teachers working together. In virtually every statement being made these days about healthy and productive organizations, or about the related topics of worker morale and development, there is direct or indirect reference to the inevitability of change and therefore the need for constant intellectual and procedural adaptation and growth. In the same vein, the workplace is defined as a working environment, and the optimal situation within the workplace is defined as collegial. Continuous interaction of workers is seen as productive of better and better-understood goals, better and better-understood means for achieving those goals, more prompt and intelligent intervention as problems arise, and better-informed decisions about the efficacy of work being done. Teachers who work closely together, instead of in isolation, therefore have far more opportunity to develop and enjoy their professional powers.

We therefore celebrate that teacher empowerment has become a strong theme in the literature and in practice, and that a variety of opportunities for partnerships with colleagues seems available. The master teacher that lurks within each of us is likelier to burst forth within the intellectual atmosphere that collegiality can create. Visualizing each school, or district office, as in effect a college (to use Zuboff's report), helps us to see that possibility more clearly. Let us think of each teaching day as a graduate seminar in which are rotated the roles of professor and learner, and therefore the academic year as a 180-day-long enrichment experience. All of us "works in progress," and all of us having the intellectual time of our lives.

Reference

Garry Emmons, "Smart Machines and Learning People," *Harvard Magazine 91*(November-December 1988), 56-60+.

Restoring Honor: A Modest Proposal

Harry S. Broudy

For those of us who have worn out yards of typewriter ribbon arguing that teaching in the public school ought to be regarded as a profession, it comes as a pleasant surprise to learn that not only has it become a profession, but that it has already lost its honorable status. Teaching has always been regarded as an honorable vocation, for like nursing it belongs to the benign helping occupations, but to be recognized as a profession is another matter.[1]

To qualify as a profession a calling must require a mastery of a body of theory that rationalizes accepted procedures for solving a special set of problems. The theories and procedures are ratified by a guild of practitioners, admission to which is formalized and regulated by the university and/or the state.

Teaching—and I take it elementary and secondary teaching is the kind these papers are about—meets these requirements. Why, then, are there questions and doubts about its professional status? Why does the criticism of these schools and their teachers so often conclude with scornful denunciations of schools of education and methods courses? Why is educational theory so low on the academic totem pole? Why are the procedures derived from it held in such low esteem? Why are "good" teachers regarded as exceptions to the rule?

To "restore" honorable *professional* status to classroom teaching—which to my mind it has never quite achieved—requires a mechanism that will utilize educational theory and practice *in the manner of a profession*. Such a mechanism is a set of paradigmatic cases that constitute the targets for the application of theory. These cases generate and regulate the education of lawyers, physicians, and accountants, and the college and university curricula responsible for it.

Teacher education (teacher training is the more usual expression) has all the ingredients for professional training *except* standardized cases. Little wonder, therefore, that despite a plentitude of research, theory, and programs of practice teaching, one cannot predict from what is going on in elementary school A what is going on in elementary school B a half mile down the road. Each district formulates sets of objectives, curricula, rules, and procedures that may or may not match those of other districts. They reflect theories and/or prejudices that may or may not correspond to those of other comparable schools. Teacher training requirements may vary from state to state, sometimes from district to district. National student examinations do tend to reduce variability, but only insofar as they promote teaching for the test.

The curricula of teacher education do exhibit a good deal of uniformity. Social, philosophical, psychological foundation courses are pretty much standard requirements, albeit the contents of these courses may vary widely. Courses in methods and classroom management are also standard components of the program, but here the variability in theory and practice covers a wide range. How wide is almost impossible to determine.

Uniformity of teacher behavior in the classroom is difficulty, if not impossible, to determine. Indeed, uniformity is often denounced as a lack of creativity. Variation on a theme can be stimulating; variations without a theme are a prescription for chaos. Creative and productive variation requires an underlying consensus on targets and generic approaches to them. Can we arrive at a set of teaching situations that could constitute such targets?

We can, of course, deduce them from an analysis of teaching. Educational theorists have been doing it since the days of the sophists. Educational history is rich in literature on curriculum instruction, organization, material, and methods of instruction.[2] It is doubtful, however, that agreements among theorists are likely if their own academic status depends on novelty, i.e., on variations without a theme. Unlike lawyers, doctors, engineers, and accountants, educationists do not confine their study to well-defined and agreed-upon problems.

Yet we do have the ingredients, both institutional and theoretical, for a profession—an honorable one. We have thousands of researchers, professors, and some 1300 colleges that profess to train teachers. We have associations and journals devoted to the study of every phase of teacher education. Despite this ferment of scholarly activity, despite the importance of the public school, the chorus of criticism of these schools, their teachers, and the teachers colleges continues unabated, reaching crescendos in every decade, resulting in a spate of reports and calls for reform.

Demands for testing teacher competence follow every national testing of their pupils. The dismal litanies of indignation at the prevalence of functional, technical, and cultural illiteracy have achieved the status of best sellers in the publishing mart. The alleged culprits include lack of family values, drugs, lack of financial support, racial discrimination, and incompetent teachers. And so the task of teaching in the public school becomes more arduous, more threatening, more stressful. Recriminations of teachers, administrators, politicians, and reformers become more shrill.

Until teachers in Montana and Rhode Island are educated to understand standard problems of instruction and be acquainted with standard literatures and methods for dealing with them, there is little hope for teaching as a profession, let alone an honorable one. For "honorable," when applied to a calling, does not refer to the moral attributes of its members, but to the respect its paradigms of diagnosis and treatment command.

Teaching will become an honorable profession when the education of teachers is grounded in certified knowledge and technical competence to deal with the problems assigned to it by the social order. But no profession, however learned and wise, can deal with the infinite variation in circumstance that characterizes human affairs until they are classified into types about which general principles can be stated and from which adaptations in practice can be deduced. Until there is consensus as to the classification of these problems and the principles relevant to their solution, there cannot be a learned profession, however learned its professors may be.

Until this comes about in teacher education, the public will not recognize teaching as a profession. Nor will examples of talented teachers alter the situation. Teachers who come up with ingenious solutions that are celebrated on television, and highly publicized demonstrations of "amateur" teachers, are witnesses to the absence of a profession rather than its existence. The professional status of a calling is not established or enhanced by the extraordinary talent of individual practitioners. Exhibitions of such individual brilliance are too rare to provide the cadre of practitioners needed by the social order. On the contrary, the more "creative" individuality is stressed, the less the validity of claims of teaching to be a profession. Medicine would not be a profession if its members were permitted to be highly creative in diagnosis and treatment. Faith healers don't hold membership in the AMA.

These considerations strongly suggest the hypothesis that teaching needs paradigm cases to which teacher education develop and apply theory and practice. These cases should be the target of foundational courses, curriculum study, methods courses, and clinical teaching.

1. About the best we can do in this situation is to determine a relatively small number of classroom situations that teachers are willing to rate as frequent in occurrence and high in urgency. Such a set (15-20) derived by a rigorously selected national sample of teachers' judgment could become the base for a set of paradigm cases.
2. These paradigm situations (cases) would then be enacted on video tape or film.
3. Research literature relevant to these cases would be formulated and made available for use with the tapes.

A team of investigators at the University of Illinois[4] has recently completed a survey to secure a national random sampling of teacher judgment on pervasive problems confronting teachers.

Armed with these data, the team has set about the task of producing video tape of the 15 situations receiving the highest ratings in the teacher survey to serve as case studies in teacher education. Each tape represents a class of situations by which every course taught in a school of education can test its relevance and to which it would be able to provide relevant fact and theory.

I shall not go into the details of the difficulties the project has encountered in securing the financial resources to carry out the production of these "cases," despite the interest it has engendered. Yet the amount needed to produce these "cases" is a tiny fraction of the money, let alone the misdirected energies, now being expended on the perennial demands for reform of the schools.

If I have placed so much faith in such a modest proposal for restoring honor to the teaching profession, it is because we have all the other ingredients for a genuinely professional cadre of classroom teachers—intelligent personnel who wish to teach, a plentitude of research, a recognized niche in the university—all the making of a learned profession, which the public will be pleased to honor.

Notes

[1]That my interest in this topic is not recent, cf. my "Teaching—Craft or Profession." *The Educational Forum, 20*:2, 1956, 175-84.

[2]H.S. Broudy and John Palmer, *Exemplars of Teaching Method.* Chicago: Rand McNally, 1965.

[3]Although I have been advocating the construction of such case studies for teacher education for several decades, implementing the venture received a powerful assist from the efforts of Dean Nancy C. Cole and Professors Steven Tozer and William Trent.

On the Art of the Practical

Elliot W. Eisner

Education today is in the early stages of a significantly new period in its history. I believe that this new period in education will, more than any other, be shaped in greater measure by those who practice education than by those who theorize it.

Two developments seem to me to be of special significance in this new period. One of these is the emerging role of teachers and school administrators in the policy-making functions of schooling. The other is our growing appreciation of the art of practice and our more measured and modest expectations of the utility of theory in the practical realm.

There are, of course, important differences between conducting a practice and having a theory of it. Theory is characteristically general and ideal. Practice is particular and ordinary. Theory is couched in language, either the language of mathematics or of propositions, and lacks of vividness that characterizes practical action. Theory is aimed at explanation and understanding. Its function is to account for what has occurred. Practice is aimed at effective decision-making. Its virtue is getting a difficult job done well. Theory takes shape in language. Practice emerges in the doing. Theory is concerned with knowing what is true. Practice is aimed at getting something done right. Theory is learned from the declaratory and the explanatory; practical knowledge is secured in the context of action. Theory must reduce what we know to statements we can test; practice depends upon knowledge that is more tacit than explicit. Theory attempts to control what confounds explanation. Practice greets the contingent as an opportunity to create new ends. Theory becomes more rigorous as its statements become increasingly formal and quantitative— detachment and standardization are among its prime operational virtues. Practice celebrates and exploits what is personal and idiosyncratic. The actor's signature, as it displays itself in its work, is a cherished feature; its absence, a liability.

These differences between theory and practice are not recited here to honor practice and to demean theory. To paraphrase Kant, theory without practice is empty and practice without theory is blind. The new appreciation of practice in the field of education is important not because it is designed to replace good theory, but because it recognizes that practitioners know more than they can tell and that the practical knowledge that they possess is not to be dismissed as some form of mystical intuition, but one of the many ways in which humans know the world in which they live.

There are no theoretical materials that can tell a second-grade teacher when a class is engaged, or a seventh-grade teacher when it is not. There is no algorithm for deciding how much wait-time is enough. Time, after all, is as much a psychological experience as it is a matter of monitoring minutes. Sixty seconds can seem like six, and six seconds can seem like sixty. We have no formulas for knowing precisely how much talk or demonstration is enough, yet skilled practitioners, those who excel at the art of teaching, seem to know quite well.

What makes such performance possible? What is it that makes it possible to regard practice as an art? To what do practitioners pay attention, and why is it, in principle, impossible to develop a technology of practice that will do for classrooms what NASA has been able to do for the moon? Finally, to what extent can the art of practice be refined and fostered, and what kinds of conditions would serve such aims? These questions will keep us occupied.

I start with the proposition that because educational practice always occurs in a context and because that context is characteristically a flux of human interactions—children dealing with tasks set by a teacher, a principal attempting to support a faculty, a superintendent wishing to get a sense of community interest—one critical ability in practice relates to the acuteness of perception that practitioners need in order to act skillfully in context. What must be noticed or seen are qualities, not simply labels. What people *mean* by their actions is located not so much in what they say, but in what they do. The meanings that pervade their doings reside in the micro-expressions of their face and hands, in their comportment, in the tone and tempo of their voice, in all the subtle and complex qualities we need to see to successfully negotiate the social world in which we live.

Knowing how to act requires knowing what a situation means, and knowing what it means requires knowing how to read a text. In this case the text is not linguistic, but qualitative. To read the text—and even the subtext of classrooms, schools, and communities—we must notice the qualities that those situations possess.

Yet noticing—that is, seeing—is clearly insufficient. The social significance of things seen requires interpretation and interpretation requires a knowledge of antecedent conditions. Yet without consciousness of the qualities to be interpreted, interpretation cannot occur.

Perception of qualities is, therefore, the first order of business in the art of practice. Without it, meanings cannot be construed.

That the perception of classrooms, schools, and communities is important for the conduct of the practical art is evident in what good teachers notice, what effective principals discern, and what skilled administrators take into account when deciding how to proceed with matters of policy and leadership. Knowing what you are dealing with is a prerequisite to skilled practical action.

The ability to know what you are dealing with depends not only upon perception, but upon sensibility. Those anesthetized to the context in which they work might be able to get away with it if they are university professors, but elementary school teachers who work with young children cannot afford the luxury of insensitivity.

Perception and the refined sensibility that makes perception acute is, in an interesting way, a kind of action. To see, or hear, or feel, we must construe or *achieve* experience. Experience is not given to us, it is taken by us, and learning how to take what is available is what we mean by perceptivity. Those whom we regard as perceptive are able to take somewhat more than the rest of us in the domain in which their perceptivity resides.

But although perception lies at the base of the art of the practical, the doing of a practical art involves making as well. The kind of making I am talking about in the context of education is making things happen. This requires a repertoire of skills. For teachers the location of these happenings is in the student's head. Unlike physicians, teachers have no pills to dispense, no injections to administer, no salves to apply. Our skills reside in making noises in the environment so that what happens to those with whom we work is beneficial. In a way, our work is closer to the work of the actor, the comedian, the dancer, and the musician than it is to those who have a license to invade the body directly to mainline their medicine. Teachers, in particular, apply this art by shaping the environment so that the interior life of the students they teach deepens and grows.

Unlike actors, musicians, and dancers, neither teachers nor school administrators have the security of a script: no curriculum guide provides a certain road to travel and despite rumors to the contrary, there are no seven sacred steps to effective teaching— there are seventy thousand. What steps to take, when, and in what order are precisely what no script can reveal. Perception is crucial for knowing what to do and when. Skilled practical action depends upon perceiving a configuration of qualities dynamically displayed in the classroom itself, or in the school, or in the community. Those whose sensibilities are tuned in have a basis for deciding. Those tuned out, have none.

So far we have identified two dimensions of the art of practice. The first is the art of sensitive perception that brings to consciousness what a practitioner needs to know in order to act. Without it, knowledge of the context is limited and the basis for action restricted. The second is the possession of a repertoire of teaching skills that can be used flexibly in response to the inevitably kaleidoscopic conditions that characterize any human enterprise. Children are not inert phenomena that one can act upon. Teaching and school administration demand a dialectical relationship with people, not merely a didactic one. If teaching is like anything analogous to music, it is closer to jazz improvisation than to the more predictable patterns of a Mozart or a Bach. Teaching profits from imagination, if for no other reason than because we can never tell when the symphony's second movement needs to begin or what the appropriate tempo should be.

The skills that constitute an educational repertoire cannot simply be applied as discrete steps within a dynamic context; they require a synthetic application and the construction of a unified whole. In artistic terms, those who make or organize form aim at coherence and, if possible, elegance and style. The art of practice aims at composing relationships that work, that fit, that are right—and this means being aware of emerging qualities, having a repertoire of skills to draw upon for action, and being able to compose in a constantly changing context. Those who can see, but who have no skills with which to act are feckless. Those who have skills, but who cannot see, are boors. Those who can compose but have no skills to bring their compositions into being are left with only dreams of the possible that are always beyond reach. These four dimensions of the art of practice can be regarded as *the perceptual*, *the interpretive*, *the constitutive*, and *the compositional*.

The perceptual makes consciousness possible. The interpretive confers meaning on what has been seen. The constitutive refers to the repertoire of skills that serve as resources for action, and the compositional to the ways in which the skills of the constitutive are related so the situation can be made whole. Because all of these elements or dimensions of practice occur in a largely unpredictable setting, imagination as well as sensibility comes into play. If teaching and educational administration could be scripted, imagination would be unnecessary and practitioners would not need to study at universities to learn about what to consider in going about their work. What practitioners learn to consider in universities is usually theoretical, but whatever educational life they lead is rooted within the art of practice. Practice is a complex art and skilled educational practice especially so.

I am convinced that improving our own practice is something that cannot be done alone: we all suffer from secondary ignorance. Primary ignorance is when you don't know something, but you know that you don't know it. Secondary ignorance is when you don't know something but you don't know that you don't know. At least some of our own behavior as people, parents, and teachers suffers from secondary ignorance, hence our need for both helpful colleagues and a school culture that fosters growth.

This brings me back to where I started, namely to matters of empowerment. My hope is that teachers and school administrators will try to shape the culture of schooling so that it honors the art of practice and provides the conditions through which it can be refined. If they are successful, the schools they shape will not only provide them with those special satisfactions that the skilled performance of any art provides, it will contribute substantively to the thousands of lives with whom they work. The art of education is one of enhancing lives. There is no art form more important nor any undertaking as delicate and complex. The time is now ripe for practitioners to move toward such heady goals. In the end it is better to find new seas upon which to sail than old ports at which to dock.

Honor Becomes Effective Teaching

Ned A. Flanders

What Teaching is Honorable?

For those of us who started our careers in education about fifty years ago it is hard to understand why it is necessary "to restore honor to teaching." We grew up honoring teachers. Just after the Great Depression, we considered a job as teacher to be highly desirable. Has the honor of teaching really eroded so much it needs to be restored? What could have happened?

The litany of woes which undermine the prestige of teaching is well documented. Gary Sykes (1983) identified six important trends, during the decade of the seventies, which "irreversibly undercut the relative attractiveness of teaching." As a result: (1) "the occupation of teaching no longer serves as a route from blue collar to white"; (2) "the occupation of teaching stands little chance of attracting the academically talented"; and (3) these two trends, in turn, will reduce the quality of teacher training at colleges and universities which prepare teachers (pp. 88-89). Sykes reluctantly concludes—

> You cannot attract a sizable number of talented college graduates to an
> occupation that features low wages, questionable working conditions,
> declining occupational prestige, declining public support, and dimin-
> ished opportunities for the exercise of professional judgement. This is
> the picture of teaching that I see in our time. (p. 93)

Even though teaching has become less attractive, there is
evidence that the morale of teachers and their perceptions of
teaching have not suffered to the same extent. Consider what
Goodlad (1983) found when he interviewed teachers about their
role and their job—

> In summary, (teachers) . . . tended to be idealistic and altruistic in their
> views of why they chose to teach. Also, the percentages expressing
> fulfillment of career expectations . . . (was) . . . quite high . . . Our date
> should make us somewhat optimistic about appealing to teachers to
> join with others in planning and conducting efforts to improve our
> schools . . . (p. 173)

In support of Goodlad's assessment of positive teacher attitudes
I would add my personal experience. During recent years, I have
had the privilege of conducting four programs designed to help
teachers analyze their own teaching in order to improve it
(Flanders, *et al.*, 1987). In one of these programs we conducted
and voice-recorded pretraining interviews in which twenty-three
teachers described their teaching priorities for this year and how
they expected to accomplish them. Our teachers worked in three
different school districts; the grade levels included primary
grades through junior high school; some worked in severely
impoverished, high crime communities and others in very weal-
thy, low crime communities; some were known to be very successful, competent teachers and others were known to be less
successful, marginal teachers; and we kept records of how each
teacher worked with a partner to analyze and improve their own

teaching. There were several kinds of questions which would be influenced by a teacher's perception of his or her role as a teacher (e.g., questions about working conditions, the support they received from parents and from administrators, etc.). No statements were recorded which could reasonably be construed as evidence that these teachers believed their profession was experiencing decreased community respect or was having or recently had its honor eroded. In addition, most teachers were proud of what they were doing, believed they were providing an essential service; in short they were showing symptoms of feeling honorable. Even teachers who were marginal in performance talked about new goals and opportunities with confidence.

How can teachers feel good about their jobs while the public and especially college students see teaching, in general, as an undesirable occupation? Teachers may find Sykes' conclusions strongly dissonant, in the sense of Festinger's (1957) theory of cognitive dissonance, and have taken steps to reduce the dissonance. Maybe teachers have found a way to isolate themselves from the view that they are in an occupation which is less honorable than in previous times. Perhaps they are so busy with current exigencies or so optimistic or so isolated they simply don't think they should have their honor restored. Their only viable option may be to ignore this erosion of confidence and isolate it from the daily chores of teaching. "Let someone else worry, I'm too busy." Given this dedication to duty, one would think that today's teachers would be accorded greater honor than in the past because they continue to work, as best they can, under conditions which, in many cases, are much worse.

We must keep in mind that not all teachers see teaching through rose colored glasses. I suppose that some small proportion of teachers, surely less than two or three percent, might pessimistically testify that teaching is indeed the pits—the dusty, dirty, noisy, isolated chalk pits. But teachers who believe this must have lost whatever rewards teaching can give. Teachers also classify teaching positions in terms of pleasant working conditions, the competence of the principal, and the congeniality of the staff. Unfortunately, some of our most competent teachers avoid the most demanding and difficult positions where they could presumably do the most good.

I believe that in education, as in all other walks of life, individuals are honored if they act honorably. I cannot believe the teaching profession has lost honor because teachers have been acting dishonorably. Therefore, there ought not to be this need to restore their honor. My faith in teachers is the product of personal contacts during my fifty years of experience as an educator, especially those years when I regularly observed classroom interaction. I certainly witnessed some excellent, artistic teaching and some abysmal, misdirected teaching. Yet the incidence of the latter, out of many hundreds of classroom visits, was small and, to the best of my knowledge, never the result of malicious intent or callous indifference. On the other hand, I would argue that at least 80 percent of all those teachers could and would have improved their teaching if they had been given the necessary opportunities and resources. Further, most of them would have participated in self-improvement programs enthusiastically if they had seen these activities as practical, rewarding, and directly applicable to their own teaching. In short, they acted in an honorable fashion.

We must be living in a new era when good intentions alone are not enough. One major change in this decade is that teachers are now being held accountable for the quality of learning in their classrooms more rigorously than in the past. Honor may be bestowed only on those who can combine good intentions with effective performance. We may have reached a point at which honor only becomes effective teachers.

Restoring Honor

The notion that we can restore honor to teaching by improving how students are taught is fraught with hazards. Consider the warning which Goodlad (*ibid.*, p. 186) wrote in his summary of teacher perceptions—

> The general picture, then, is of teachers viewing themselves as well prepared in their subjects (with some exceptions at the elementary school level) and their colleagues as performing well. One wonders if these teachers would respond with alacrity to proposals for school improvement focused primarily on the need to upgrade teachers' qualifications and current effectiveness. My conclusion is that they would not.

Goodlad also points out that the problems which confront schools can be quite different, one school compared to another. This suggests that each school would have different priorities. Teachers would be most likely to participate in programs to improve education if they had a strong voice in identifying the problems to be addressed and helped to design the procedures to be carried out in their own school. How administrators in a particular school create opportunities for genuine teacher participation would determine, to a large extent, the success of the program. Teachers will want to become full fledged partners in the design and conduct of school improvement programs, but only if their current responsibilities can be reduced so that the time, space, and resources required by the task can be made available.

To realize how difficult a schoolwide approach may be, it is instructive to turn to Goodlad's study once again. His discussion of teacher isolation, on pages 187-88, is quite provocative:

> The teachers in our sample ... rarely joined with peers in collaborative endeavors such as district committees or projects. Nor did they visit other schools or receive visitors from them very often. There was little in our data to suggest active, ongoing exchanges of ideas and practices across schools, between groups of teachers, or between individuals even in the same schools. Teachers rarely worked together on school-wide problems ...

> Inside schools, teacher-to-teacher links for mutual assistance in teaching or collaborative school improvement were weak or nonexistent, especially in the senior high schools. Most teachers taught alone in a classroom. A large majority said they never observed instruction in other classrooms ...

> The very nature and conduct of the schooling enterprise appear to operate against the concept of principals, teachers, parents, and perhaps students working together on schoolwide problems ... Schools ... are not infrastructures designed to encourage or support either communication among teachers in improving their teaching or collaboration in attacking schoolwide problems ... It will require more than exhortation to change this situation.

To the extent Goodlad is right, one might begin by gradually developing effective communication on topics which represent the highest priorities of teachers. Since the quality of small group participation depends on skillful participation, teachers will need a chance to practice and nurture their communication skills. When problem priorities are to be discussed, careful preparation might include identifying faculty leaders, training them as discussion leaders, establishing agenda based on the suggestions of teachers, and making sure that teachers have a good opportunity to influence the proceedings if that is their wish.

Let me end these comments with a reminder of what might be called the teachers' locus of control. If teacher participation in activities designed to improve education is to be successful, it should deal with tasks over which teachers exert control. These are problems, tasks, or programs which occur within the school and its immediate environment.

References

Festinger, Leon (1957). *A Theory of Cognitive Dissonance.* Evanston, IL: Row, Peterson.

Flanders, Ned A. (1987). (With J.B. Bowyer, R.C. Ponzio, Lawrence Ingvarson, R.P. Tisher, L.F. Lowery, and Karen Reynolds) Support systems for teachers who form partnerships to help each other improve teaching. *Teacher Education Quarterly,* Summer 1987, v. 14, #3.

Goodlad, John I. (1984). *A Place Called School: Prospects for the Future.* NY: McGraw-Hill.

Sykes, Gary (1983). Contradictions, ironies, and promises unfulfilled: a contemporary account of the status of teaching. *Phi Delta Kappan,* October 1983, v. 65, #2.

Final Thoughts

The last collection of essays are important as they address concerns which permeate our profession. John Hope Franklin reminds us of the need to attract and keep minority teachers. William Friday provides suggestions on how a community can help to renew and reinvigorate teachers. Theodore Hesburgh provides us with a perspective from the private education sector. Those of us in public education forget, sometimes, the important role private education plays in the total educational endeavors of this country.

The Desperate Need for Black Teachers

John Hope Franklin

No group in the United States has manifested a consistently greater interest in and respect for education than black Americans. Undoubtedly, the fact that education was withheld from them for more than two centuries must have aroused their curiosity about it and stimulated their desire to secure it at all costs. After slavery, when they flocked to schools in huge numbers, some whites asserted that it was a fad in which they would soon lose interest. This proved not to be the case, however, and blacks continued to value education and to go to school in increasing numbers in the nineteenth and twentieth centuries. They did so in the face of a growing disparity between funds spent for the education of black and white children, and even in the face of threats and intimidation designed to discourage black children from attending school.

Just as school attendance became popular among black Americans, many young trained black men and women began to

This article originally appeared in *Change*, May/June 1987, pp. 44-45.

pursue teaching as a career. The fact that they were barred because of race from many exciting careers in business, industry, and the professions did not diminish the honor or the importance of teaching, as they viewed it. Perhaps even because their opportunities were so tragically limited, it appears that black teachers became unusually determined and deeply committed to their profession. The result was that in public and private secondary schools and in historically black colleges, teaching standards rose, thanks to the rigorous teaching and unremitting dedication of the black teacher. Whether it was at the public Dunbar High School in Washington, or the private Palmer Memorial institute in North Carolina, or many dozens of institutions for young black students across the nation, the results led to the graduation of a procession of remarkable young black Americans who made their mark in life in a variety of commendable ways.

Thus, teaching became and remained an honorable and revered profession among black Americans. Even as new opportunities lured some teachers into areas from which they had been barred for generations, others resisted the temptation and remained in the schools to train the young people who presented themselves. Indeed, there are literally thousands of teachers who, for no reason other than commitment and dedication, have remained at their posts, ignoring the blandishments and attractions offered in other fields. Their work through the years is one of the exciting and untold stories in the field of education.

Even so, the teachers who remain are not sufficient to meet the demand. Students themselves continue to increase in number. Curriculums continue to increase in complexity, demanding specialties hitherto unanticipated. Temptations persist, and the attrition in the number of black teachers who opt for other careers continues. It is now painfully clear that teaching, once the bulwark of professional life among black Americans and an important factor in their ongoing educational strivings, is declining in appeal. The consequences of this can be devastating. If it continues it will mean not only that blacks will drop out of one of the oldest and most honored professions, but also that young blacks will be deprived of the role models and a special kind of caring that are essentially irreplaceable. And the drop-out rate among them will continue.

It is not often that one finds it desirable to turn back the clock, but in this instance it would be a very happy eventuality. We need to return to the situation in which teaching is so attractive that it will once again draw in vast numbers of able, dedicated, committed black teachers. We need to do everything possible to retain young blacks in secondary schools and beyond. Otherwise, they will be recruits for more unemployment and greater marginality. The need for black teachers has reached the point of desperation. The need for black students to remain in school has gone even beyond that point. Consequently, the trend in both areas must be stopped if we are to see anything resembling a healthy attitude toward—and respect for—education in the black community.

Professional Renewal and Restoring Honor to the Profession of Teaching

William Friday

It has long been clear to me that teaching is at once the most difficult and the most honorable of professions. We have all been touched by the example, guidance, and motivation of a teacher whose often reluctant pupil we were. We can each recall a moment of insight or truth when caught in the act of learning. None of us owe larger debts for whatever we may have become, for whatever we may have been able to accomplish, than we owe to teachers in our past lives whose total devotion to young people and to their discipline has been their chief reward and the reason we honor teachers and the teaching profession.

Now, in the midst of the third decade of educational reform, we share serious concern for the impairments we see in the role and perception of teaching and our teachers. Dozens of national reports have called for major revisions in our methods of preparing teachers, in recruitment procedures, in conditions of teaching, and for restoring prestige and honor to what has become a threatened profession.

One need not search too far to note that the surroundings in which teachers work, especially in large urban schools and in small rural areas, are difficult, to say the least. I continue to marvel at the stream of intelligent and highly motivated teachers who are drawn to the profession and who perform admirably in adverse conditions. Yet fewer will come to the profession and more will leave the profession early if steps are not taken to restore order, honor and public support for teachers.

Certainly, state legislators, governors and boards of education must address the matter of competitive salaries for teachers, the conditions of work in the schools must be improved, and more must be done to recruit the best into teacher education programs and into the profession. I am heartened by the many steps being taken to improve these three major factors in my own North Carolina and in other states around the nation.

However, among others, there are at least three other kinds of initiatives that must be taken to strengthen teachers, to reposition the schools to provide education for today's society, and to restore honor and integrity to the teaching profession.

First, I believe that there is no more important mission for a university than to prepare teachers for the public schools. As a matter of policy, each university must commit a major share of its resources to the preparation of classroom teachers and must see its own integrity and effectiveness in light of the quality of the teachers it produces. The "prestige gap" between high school and college teaching that has arisen since the 1960s must be closed and a seamless web of education must be created that restores the integrity that teaching once held as a profession that is equally honored at all levels. The many school-college partner-ship programs that have been formed throughout the country are heartening evidence that closing this gap might be accomplished in the near future.

Second, teachers must have strong administrative support and aggressive, positive leadership. Principals and other school administrators must themselves be outstanding educational leaders and managers who command the respect of teachers, who will share planning and educational decision-making power with teachers, and who will evaluate teachers fairly and with objective means. I am impressed by the "lead-teachers" projects springing up around my own state and with the steps that have been taken to reform programs for preparing senior school administrators and for providing better access to leadership training and career development opportunities for those who wish to remain in the classroom without foregoing economic and reputational advancement.

Third, teaching requires regular intellectual stimulation and personal professional renewal. Perhaps the most unique activity developed to meet this need is a cooperative program of the university and the public schools in North Carolina. In 1986, the North Carolina Center for the Advancement of Teaching was established in the western mountain region of our state in Cullowhee. The purpose of this Center is to provide reward, renewal and rededication opportunities for career classroom teachers in the public schools of North Carolina. It is not a traditional in-service teacher training program. No credit is earned. There are no tests or certification requirements. It is an intellectually renewing five-day experience that includes interdisciplinary seminars, intellectual exploration, and collegial debate. In groups of 20, teachers recommended for Center seminars revisit their own intellectual interests, work closely with peers and redevelop the perspective on education and on themselves that brought them to the profession.

It is at once an anti-burnout program, an invigorating educational and social experience, and a re-charging professional event that is igniting hundreds of teachers in our state. Thus far, nearly 1,000 teachers have been Center scholars and the new facilities being completed in the Carolina mountain setting will serve many more in the future.

For honor to be restored to the teaching profession, it must be earned and preserved. It cannot be conferred. But the conditions must be restored and strengthened that allow teaching to be viewed as a profession with integrity and that provide teachers with a self-concept and the competence required to maintain professional status.

For that restoration to occur, the resources and support of the university must be added to the efforts of legislators, school boards and teacher associations to improve the lot of teachers, there must be a concerted effort made to maintain a high level of educational leadership, and there must be clear dedication to the treatment of teachers as professional persons of integrity and the provision of opportunities for teachers to regularly achieve personal-professional renewal.

How to Enhance the Role of Teachers

Theodore M. Hesburgh

How does one enhance the role of the teacher in our day? Just posing the question presumes that we have a problem and indeed we do—in fact, several.

Good teachers are generally underpaid, while we put up with bad ones who are overpaid for what they do. Bad teachers are not born, they are developed by poor education that leaves them unprepared or, worse, badly prepared.

Then there are the conditions of teaching that so often leave much to be desired: overcrowded classrooms, uninspiring curricula, unchallenging materials, unruly behavior of students, endemic truancy, low aspirations of all involved, not just students, but parents, administrators, and associates, too.

Having said all this, may I say that there are still great teachers, great schools, and great students, too. I admit to being spoiled because at Notre Dame where the students are among the upper five per cent of all high school graduates, good teaching is not only required; if not demonstrated, there is no future on this faculty. As for discipline, the students generally want to learn, attend class regularly, do their assigned work, behave extraordinarily well (except on some Saturday nights after home football games); and if all this is not true, they are not around long. Even so, we always lose less than one per cent of the freshman class. The facilities, classrooms, laboratories, library, computers, faculty offices and faculty club are good and getting better. So is the pay.

I say all this because it seems important to start off positively, to demonstrate that good teaching is possible, honorable, and self-fulfilling. The problem is what to do when it is not.

Obviously, it is a matter of national, state, and local priorities. When we demand excellence in every material thing, food, drink, accommodations, and transportation, for example, why not demand excellence of our educational systems and those at the heart of the system, the teachers?

There is no excuse whatever for poor facilities, poor support, poor recompense and recognition for teachers in the wealthiest country in history. We will not continue to be the best unless we demand the best educational system and support, whatever it needs to be the best.

What is needed for this is first to make teaching a cherished and honored profession so that it will attract the best people. Once attracted, they must be fully supported. In our society, we do this best by paying them adequately. But they also require a wide variety of back-up support in the matter of facilities, good curricula, assured discipline that begins at home and continues in the classroom.

I wish I knew more about the proper education for teachers, but I have the impression that our university departments of education, with a few exceptions, tend to be the weakest and least demanding departments, where everyone gets a doctorate of generally low academic esteem. I am of little help on advice here, since all I did was negative; I closed down our Department of

Education. It would have been better if I had reopened it in a new and exciting and demanding reincarnation. But I didn't, and I regret that, because without first rate departments of education, we are unlikely to get first rate teachers, at least in our elementary and secondary schools where they are desperately needed and in short supply.

I have one other observation that speaks to our problem. America has always been torn between two great, but often conflicting ideals: quality and equality. It would be relatively easy to maintain high standards, if one were to educate only the elite in the nation—as some European countries did. However, the best and the brightest are not always and never exclusively just that. Talent is where it is found and it is found everywhere. This is what makes America great; we aspire for both quality and equality of education simultaneously. A good education for all is our goal.

We are not quite there. Most of our best schools are in our most affluent neighborhoods and most of our poor schools are in the ghettos. This means that our best teachers are not where they are most needed. There are a variety of well-known reasons for this—but we are not achieving the goal we profess, both quality and equality.

The answer? Maybe we should create very large city schools, as we have created the campuses of our great state universities. We know from these universities how to create a large and efficient teaching environment that services as many as forty or fifty thousand students.

There would be several special advantages in this for teachers. This would be a new and secure environment. All good teachers could have sections of various types of students: the slow, the average, and the very best. The support facilities would be the newest and the best. And, hopefully, the school would operate eleven months a year which would mean higher salaries. Also, by using the latest television and computer techniques, the very best teachers in the school could be presented to all the students on an experimental basis that might eventually provide enormous economies of scale and salaries for the best that would equal star performers elsewhere.

All this would greatly enhance the role of teachers in our day and greatly benefit students and society as well.